WHAT'S YOUR NAME, AGAIN?

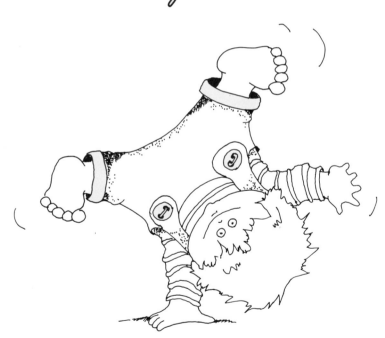

Make Me Laugh!

WHAT'S YOUR NAME, AGAIN?

more jokes about names

by Rick & Ann Walton / pictures by Joan Hanson

Lerner Publications Company · Minneapolis

To Colleen, who's neat

This book is available in two editions:
Library binding by Lerner Publications Company
Soft cover by First Avenue Editions
241 First Avenue North
Minneapolis, Minnesota 55401

Library of Congress Cataloging-in-Publication Data

Walton, Rick.
   What's your name, again?

   (Make me laugh!)
   Summary: More jokes about names such as "What
do you call a girl who babbles? Brooke."
   1. Names, Personal—Juvenile humor. 2. Wit and
humor, Juvenile. [1.Names. Personal—Wit and
humor. 2. Jokes] I. Walton, Ann, 1963-   . II. Hanson,
Joan, ill. III. Title. IV. Series.
PN6231.N24W35   1988   818'.5402   87-22634
ISBN 0-8225-0997-0 (lib. bdg.)
ISBN 0-8225-9553-2 (pbk.)

Manufactured in the United States of America

   2   3   4   5   6   7   8   9   10   97   96   95   94   93   92   91   90   89

Q: Who drinks up all the water in the bathtub?

A: Dwayne.

Q: What do you call a boy who finds gold?
A: Rich.

Q: Who has only one cent to her name?
A: Penny.

Q: Who doesn't have five cents to his name?
A: Nicolas.

Q: Who *does* have five cents to her name?
A: Nicole.

Q: Who can you put in your pocket?
A: Minnie.

Q: Who never pays back the money he borrows?

A: Owen.

Q: Who borrows money from banks and doesn't pay it back?

A: Robin.

Q: Who throws things?

A: Chuck.

Q: Who has to comb his arms?
A: Harry.

Q: What do you call two people who are looking for a contact lens?

A: Hans and Denise.

Q: Who goes a long way?

A: Miles.

Q: Who has a spring in her step?

A: May.

Q: Who uses binoculars?

A: Seymour.

Q: What do you call a boy with big eyes?
A: Luke.

Q: What do you call the person you're talking to?

A: Hugh.

Q: Who agrees with everything?

A: Kay.

Q: What do you call a girl who talks up a storm?

A: Gail.

Q: Who doesn't know where she's going?
A: Wanda.

Q: What do you call a boy who's always sunny?

A: Ray.

Q: Who makes your skin turn brown?

A: Tanya.

Q: Who knows where to find oil?

A: Derrick.

Q: Who lives on the beach?

A: Sandy.

Q: Who likes to catch fish?
A: Annette.

Q: What do you call a boy who's crackers?
A: Graham.

Q: Who is covered in sugar glaze and bobs up and down in a cup of hot chocolate?
A: Duncan.

Q: Who has a wet face and an apple in his mouth?
A: Bob.

Q: Who's clumsy with knives?
A: Nick.

Q: Who leaves the ballpark because people keep hitting him?

A: Homer.

Q: Who do you send where you don't want to go?

A: Hugo.

Q: What do you call a driver who doesn't look where he's going?

A: Rex.

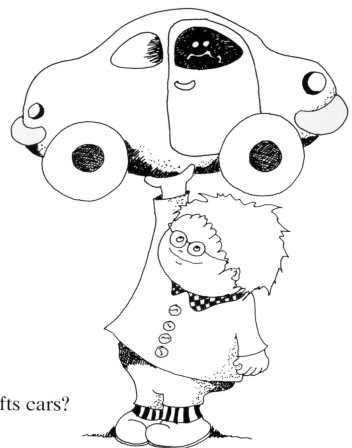

Q: Who lifts cars?
A: Jack.

Q: What do you call a girl who babbles?
A: Brooke.

Q: Who has been out in the rain for too long?
A: Rusty.

Q: Who lies across rivers and lets cars drive over her?
A: Bridget.

Q: Who falls off his raft into shallow
water?
A: Wade.

Q: Who do people step on before they go into the house?

A: Matt.

Q: Who falls into the fireplace and goes up the chimney?

A: Ashley.

Q: Who is a good housekeeper?

A: Dustin.

Q: On what girl do people hang their coats?

A: Peg.

Q: What do you call a boy who makes your voice louder?

A: Mike.

Q: What do you call a bookworm?

A: Reed.

Q: What do you call a boy who bothers you like a pesky insect?

A: Nat.

Q: Who likes to draw on you and me?
A: Marcus.

Q: What do you call a cowboy with a hot iron?

A: Brandon.

Q: Who has a colt and is a little hoarse?

A: Winnie.

Q: Who always has a cold?

A: Isaac.

Q: What girl is just purr-fect?

A: Kitty.

Q: Who has a mean cat that scratches all over his face?

A: Claude.

Q: What do you call a girl who's chicken?
A: Henny.

Q: Who is good at indoor sports?
A: Jim.

Q: Who has a ring to his name?
A: Abel.

Q: Whose father is a letter of the alphabet?
A: Jason.

Q: Who comes in a box in several pieces?
A: Kit.

ABOUT THE AUTHORS

RICK AND ANN WALTON love to read, travel, play guitar, study foreign languages, and write for children. Rick also collects books and writes music while Ann knits and does origami. They are both graduates of Brigham Young University and live in Provo, Utah, where Rick teaches sixth grade.

ABOUT THE ARTIST

JOAN HANSON lives with her husband and two sons in Afton, Minnesota. Her distinctive, deliberately whimsical pen-and-ink drawings have illustrated more than 30 children's books. Hanson is also an accomplished weaver. A graduate of Carleton College, Hanson enjoys tennis, skiing, sailing, reading, traveling, and walking in the woods surrounding her home.

Make Me Laugh!